1 One

MW01107729

There is no power in a charm
That dangles from a chain,
Nor could a wooden statue help
If we were feeling pain.
We wouldn't wave a magic wand
To get our daily bread,
Nor could a rabbit's foot give us
Our clothes and comfy bed.
Because there is but one true Lord
Who blesses us each day,
We do not worship idols, but
To Him we only pray.

1

2 Two

When God created the earth, He said, "Let there be lights in the sky to separate the day from the night." Write the first letter of each picture on the line above it to see what God made for us.

During the day we see the

_____   _____   _____

During the night we see the

_____   _____   _____   _____

Two Make a Pair

Loud thunder boomed and lightning streaked
Through storm clouds thick and dark,
As two by two they filed aboard
Old Noah's mighty ark.

Draw lines to match the animals that are the same.

3 Three

When baby Jesus was born, God put a special star in the sky. The Wise Men from far away followed this star to find Jesus and Mary and Joseph in Bethlehem. Solve the riddles to find out the three gifts that the Wise Men brought. Ask an adult to help you read Matthew 2 if you need help.

I was a Wise Man's special gift

To Jesus at His birth,

For I'm that yellow metal that

Some people say has worth.

But there is nothing on this earth—

No, nothing to behold—

More precious than God's truth and love,

Especially, not ―――――――――

A Treat for the Nose

Long ago folks peeled the bark

From off a certain tree.

Then they dug into its trunk

In order to get me.

I was used as incense, for

My resin smelled so sweet

When people placed me over flames,

Exposing me to heat.

You know me as a Wise Man's gift—

Now I was one of three.

My name begins with letter *F*

And ends with letter *E*.

_____

One More Gift for Jesus

I'm a sticky resin that

Is similar to gum,

But if you chewed me, I'd taste bad—

You'd never say, "Yum-yum!"

Although I have a bitter taste,

I really smell quite nice.

King Solomon said I smelled sweet,

Just like a pungent spice.

The book of Matthew says when Christ

Was born in Bethlehem,

The Wise Men brought me as a gift.

My name begins with *M*.

_____

Three Sons

God told Noah to build a big ark to keep his family and some animals safe during a great flood that covered the entire earth. Noah had three sons. Their names were Ham, Shem, and Japheth. Find and circle their names in the boxes.

4 Four

On the fourth day of creation, God created beautiful lights in the sky.

The moon that lights the darkest night,
And stars that twinkle, oh, so bright!
The cheerful sun that warms each day—
Thank You, God, for light, we pray.

Circle the things that God placed in the sky.

Four Small Creatures

God's Word tells us about four creatures that are small, but very wise. Unscramble the letters to spell each creature's name.

This creature has little strength, but stores up its food in the summer. N T A

_____

This creature has little power, but makes its home among rugged rocks. A D G E R B

_____

This creature has no king or leader, yet travels in an orderly way with others of its kind.

C U S T L O

_____

This creature can be caught with the hand, yet it can be found in king's palaces.

L I Z D R A

_____

5 Five

When Joseph was governor of Egypt, his brothers traveled to Egypt to get food. Joseph gave each of them gifts, including a set of clothes. To his young brother, Benjamin, he gave *five* sets of clothes. Circle the types of clothes that Joseph might have given to Benjamin.

The Fifth Day

On the fifth day of creation, God created all the creatures that swim in the seas and rivers. He also created all the birds that fly in the sky.

Follow the directions to make burlap place mats for each member of your family. Decorate them with fish and birds.

Materials

1 or 2 burlap bags or pieces of burlap fabric
Scissors
Liquid tempera paint
Shellac spray in an aerosol can

Cut pieces of material the size of a place mat from the burlap. Paint a fish or bird on each mat. (Do not mix water with the tempera paint when painting on burlap.)

After the paint dries, ask an adult to help you spray each mat with shellac. (Use shellac outside or in a properly-ventilated room.) If you wish, pull two or three threads from each side of the mat to make a fringe.

Sweet Things

In Bible times there was no sugar. People used honey to sweeten their food. Count the desserts. How many did you count?

_____

Circle the picture that does not belong.

Solve the Riddle

When it is warm, just freshly baked,

Yum-yum, does it smell good!

Slice after slice, you'll eat it up.

I have no doubt you could.

When it was baked in flattened loaves,

The Bible folks it fed.

Barley, wheat, and spelt were ground

To make this food called

_____

Jesus fed over 5,000 people with only
five loaves of this food and two fish.

6 Six

On the sixth day of creation, God created all the animals that live on land. God also created Adam and Eve in His own image. Circle the things that live on land.

Six Homes

Underline the six homes mentioned in this poem.

Buzzy bees like beehives, and

Warm caves are nice for bears.

Lions snuggle down to sleep

In cozy dens called lairs.

Inside their igloos, Eskimos

Keep warm and do not freeze,

And crawly spiders spin their webs,

And fish live in God's seas.

When Jesus lived on earth, most people lived in very small houses built by groups of neighbors. A house had one square room made of bricks of dried mud mixed with straw. The bricks were formed in wooden molds and placed in the sun to dry. Mud was used to hold the bricks together, and to cover the finished walls.

15

Who Lives in These Six Homes?

Draw a line from each animal or person to its home.

7 Seven

After God created the heavens and the earth, He blessed the seventh day and made it holy. On this day He rested from all the work He had done. We remember this day by praising God, reading His Word, and resting. Connect the dots to see where we like to go on Sunday.

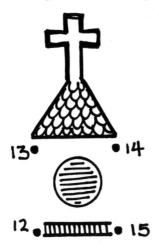

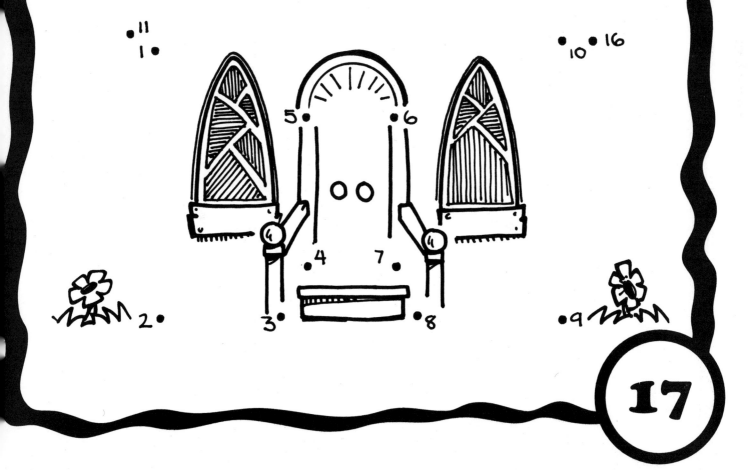

8 Eight

When God created ocean fish
In colors and in stripes,
He also made a creature with
Long arms like curling pipes.

How many arms does this creature have? _____

Print the first letter of each picture on the lines to learn the name of this creature.

A Shepherd Boy

A man called Jesse had eight sons;
The youngest grew to fame
As a shepherd boy who had
Uncommonly good aim.
He killed a giant with a stone
Slung from his shepherd's sling,
And when he grew to manhood, he
Became a famous king.

David was not afraid to face Goliath. He knew God would protect him,
just as he protected the sheep in his father's flock. How many sheep are in
the picture?

_____

19

Thank You, God, for Snow

I picked a snowflake from the ground—
So white, so tiny, and so round.
I quickly caught one in the air,
But this seemed to be quite square.
Then I thought to play a game
Of finding flakes that were the same.
One had two eyes just like a face,
And some were patterns in fine lace.
Among the thousands lying there,
I *finally* found a matching pair.

Draw a line between the eight pairs of snowflakes that match.

Make a Snowflake

Start with a square piece of paper. Follow these steps to make a snowflake. (Omit the sixth step to make a six-pointed star.)

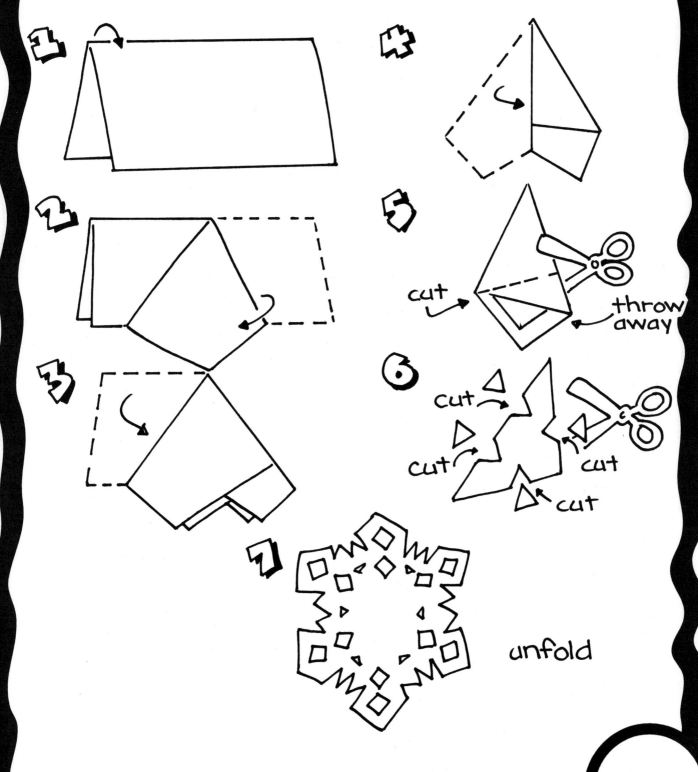

9 Nine

Remember shepherd David who
Grew up to be a king?
When he was just a lad, he killed
That giant with a sling.
The army of the Israelites
Stood back and watched in fright
As David killed this Philistine
Who stood nine feet in height.

Discover the name of this giant by printing the first letter of each picture on the line above it.

Thank You, God, for Clothes to Keep Us Warm

Pictured below are nine mittens. Match the pairs. Then draw the *lost* mitten.

10 Ten

The Ten Commandments God gave us—
His laws by which to live;
But if we often disobey,
Because of Jesus, He'll forgive.

Talk with an adult about some of the ways you can keep each commandment to show your love for God and each other.

1. You shall have no other gods.

2. You shall not misuse the name of the Lord your God.

3. Remember the Sabbath day by keeping it holy.

4. Honor your father and your mother.

5. You shall not murder.

6. You shall not commit adultery.

7. You shall not steal.

8. You shall not give false testimony against your neighbor.

9. You shall not covet your neighbor's house.

10. You shall not covet your neighbor's wife, or his manservant or maidservant, his ox or donkey, or anything that belongs to your neighbor.

Jesus Helps Me

We can't keep the commandments perfectly all by ourselves. When we sin and disobey a commandment, we tell God and the person we hurt that we are sorry and ask them to forgive us. God forgives us because Jesus took our punishment on the cross. He sends His Holy Spirit to help us follow His commandments. For the next ten days, have your family help you write down times when you notice one another sharing God's love and following His commandments.

Moses on Mt. Sinai

Moses climbed Mount Sinai
And there he stood in awe,
While God spoke face-to-face with him
And handed down His law.

Draw a line through the maze to help Moses climb to the top of the mountain.

11 Eleven

In Bible times, breakfast was usually a snack of dried fruit carried and eaten on the way to work. Lunch might have been bread and olives, and possibly, a piece of fruit. For most families, the evening meal was a vegetable stew, with a piece of bread used as a spoon to dip into a common pot.

Count the spoons. How many do you see? _____

Circle the spoon that does not have a partner with a matching design.

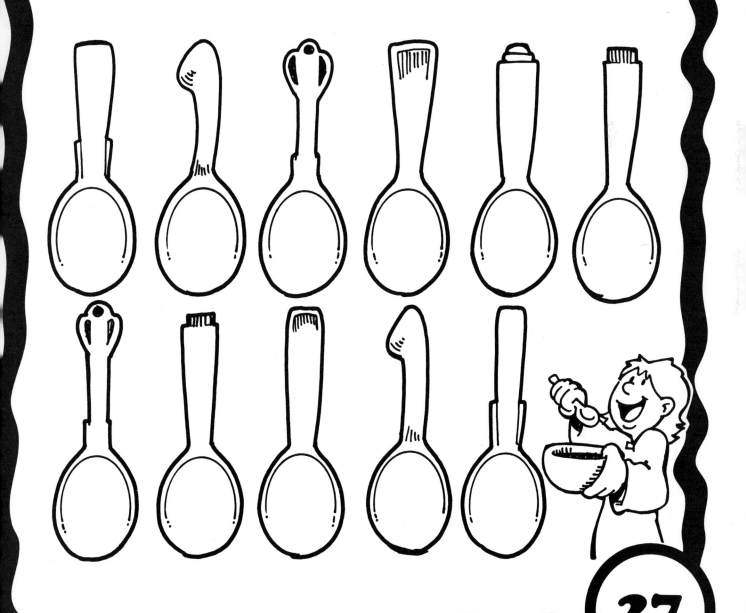

12 Twelve

Joseph had a dream that the sun, moon, and eleven stars bowed down to him. First connect the dots. Then count how many stars you see.

Food in a Shell

Eggs were poached in olive oil
By Bible folks back then,
And even now they're valued as
That product of the hen.

We decorate eggs at Eastertime because eggs and baby chicks remind us of the new life we have in Jesus. Because we believe Jesus died for us on the cross and rose again, we will live with Him forever in heaven one day. Decorate the 12 eggs to celebrate the Good News we know about Easter.

Twelve Disciples

Ask an adult to help you use these clues to fill in the crossword puzzle on page 31. (If you need help, find the answer in the Bible passage.)

ACROSS

2. Until this disciple saw the risen Christ, he doubted. (John 21:24–28)

3. This disciple betrayed Jesus. (Matthew 10:4)

5. At the last supper, this disciple asked Jesus to show them His father. "Whoever has seen Me," Jesus said, "has seen the Father." What is the name of this disciple? (John 14:8)

7. Jesus nicknamed this disciple and his brother, James, "Sons of Thunder." (Mark 3:17)

8. This disciple was a tax collector before Jesus said, "Follow Me." God also inspired him to write the first Gospel. (Matthew 9:9)

9. Like his brother, John, this disciple was a fisherman. (Matthew 4:21)

10. This fisherman's name mean's "rock." Andrew was his brother. (Matthew 16:18)

DOWN

1. This man from Cana had the longest name of all the disciples. It begins with a *B*. (Matthew 10:3)

2. Although he was a faithful follower, little is known about this disciple whose name begins with a *T*. (Matthew 10:3)

4. This disciple's name began with an *S*. He was called "the Zealot." (Matthew 10:4)

6. Jesus called this fisherman and his brother, Peter, to be His disciples. This disciple's name begins with *A*. (Matthew 10:2)

9. This disciple was younger than the other disciple who shared the same name.(Matthew 10:3)

THOMAS
JUDAS
THADDAEUS
BARTHOLOMEW
MATTHEW
PHILIP   JAMES
SIMON ANDREW JOHN
JAMES
PETER

Follow Me

Twelve disciples Jesus had,
They followed Him each day,
Because they knew He was God's Son,
The Truth, the Light, the Way.

Counting

By now we've counted 1 through 12.
What fun we've had today,
We learned about God's numbers and
God's world along the way.

Solve this riddle to find something with 12 numbers.

My hands have no fingers. My stem cannot grow.
And 'though I lack legs, I can run fast or slow.
I tell you to hurry, or tell you to wait—
For I let you know if you're early or late.
Draw a picture of the answer—with 12 numbers!